Although every effort has been made to ensure that website addresses are correct at time of going to press, Hodder Education cannot be held responsible for the content of any website mentioned in this book. It is sometimes possible to find a relocated web page by typing in the address of the home page for a website in the URL window of your browser.

Hachette UK's policy is to use papers that are natural, renewable and recyclable products and made from wood grown in well-managed forests and other controlled sources. The logging and manufacturing processes are expected to conform to the environmental regulations of the country of origin.

To order, please visit www.hoddereducation.com or contact Customer Service at education@hachette.co.uk / +44 (0)1235 827827.

ISBN: 978 1 0360 0703 4

© Tess Bayley 2024

First published in 2023 by Hodder Education,
An Hachette UK Company
Carmelite House
50 Victoria Embankment
London EC4Y 0DZ

www.hoddereducation.com

Impression number   10 9 8 7 6 5 4 3 2

Year   2027 2026 2025 2024

All rights reserved. Apart from any use permitted under UK copyright law, no part of this publication may be reproduced or transmitted in any form or by any means, electronic or mechanical, including photocopying and recording, or held within any information storage and retrieval system, without permission in writing from the publisher or under licence from the Copyright Licensing Agency Limited. Further details of such licences (for reprographic reproduction) may be obtained from the Copyright Licensing Agency Limited, www.cla.co.uk

Cover photo © fizkes - stock.adobe.com

Illustrations by Integra Software Services Pvt. Ltd., Pondicherry, India

Typeset in India

Printed and bound in Great Britain by Bell and Bain Ltd, Glasgow

A catalogue record for this title is available from the British Library.

Contents

	Introduction	4
1	Business context part 1: sections 1.1–1.6	5
2	Business context part 2: sections 1.7–1.11	16
3	People	30
4	Quality and compliance	40
5	Finance	49
6	Policies and procedures	61
7	Project and change management	70
8	Business behaviours	82

Answers can be found online at www.hoddereducation.com

Management and Administration T Level Exam Practice Workbook

Introduction

This workbook will help you to prepare to tackle exam questions for the core component of the T Level Technical Qualification in Management and Administration (8715).

The two exams covered by this book are both 2.5 hours long and are worth 100 marks each. Each externally set paper forms 30 per cent of the overall core grade.

The following topics are covered in each exam:

Paper 1
- Unit 1 Business context
- Unit 2 People
- Unit 7 Business behaviours

Paper 2
- Unit 3 Quality and compliance
- Unit 4 Finance
- Unit 5 Policies and procedures
- Unit 6 Project and change management

Both exams include a range of short-answer and extended-response questions.

Features to help you succeed

Each topic area starts with **recall activities** that will help you to remember important information you will need when answering exam questions. These activities include crosswords, quizzes, matching exercises and filling in missing words in tables, sentences or diagrams.

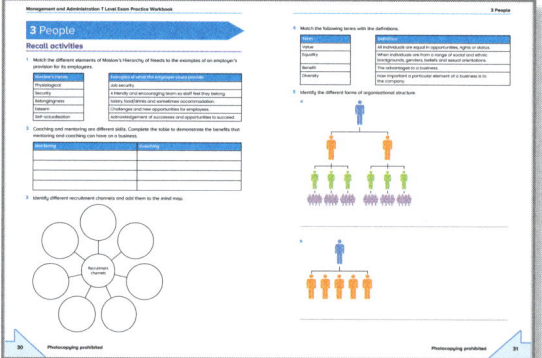

Short-answer exam practice questions help you to practise answering multiple-choice and short-answer exam questions that are typically worth 1–4 marks.

Longer-answer exam practice questions will help you to practise answering extended-response questions typically worth 6–12 marks. These questions will usually include a context or scenario.

Some short-answer and longer-answer questions include **hints** next to them to give you extra advice on how to approach the question. They may suggest key points to consider when answering the question, explain what important words included in the question mean, or give guidance on common mistakes candidates make when answering these types of questions.

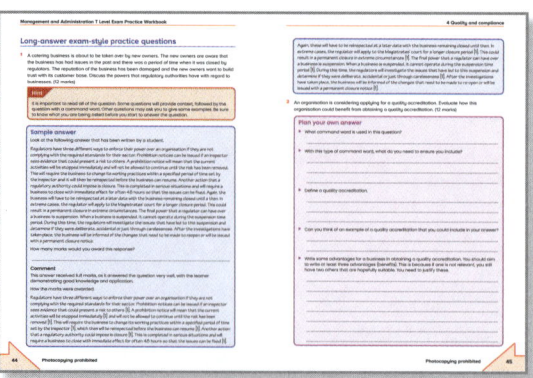

Some questions will also include guidance to support you as you answer the question. They may identify and explain **command** words for you, or have bullet points or mind maps for you to complete to help you to plan and structure your answer.

Sample student answers are provided for some questions. These will help you understand how to gain the most marks, and may ask you to think about the strengths and weaknesses of the answer and how it could be improved.

All questions will have spaces for you to write and plan your answers.

1 Business context part 1: sections 1.1–1.6

Recall activities

1. Match the following terms to their definitions.

Term	Description
Private sector	This consists of non-profit-making organisations.
Voluntary sector	This part of the economy is organised and controlled by the government.
Public sector	Organisations within the economy that are owned by individuals or groups of individuals.
Charity	An organisation that benefits the public but does not make any profit.
Non-governmental organisations (NGOs)	An organisation that maximises profits to provide social value.
Charity commission	A government body that regulates and registers charities in England and Wales.
Social enterprise	Organisations that are separate from the government and which are not commercial or profit-making.

2. Sort the following organisations into one of the following categories:

   ▷ Royal British Legion
   ▷ NHS
   ▷ Thames Water
   ▷ Environmental Agency
   ▷ Centre Parcs UK
   ▷ Office for National Statistics
   ▷ Co-op
   ▷ Oxfam
   ▷ The National Lottery
   ▷ Community Fund
   ▷ Arsenal FC
   ▷ Marks and Spencer PLC

Private sector	Public sector	Voluntary sector

3   Look at the descriptions of different businesses and determine if they belong to the private, public or voluntary sector.

Term	Description
Private sector	To address an issue/need and to provide goods and/or services that may have been neglected by other sectors.
Public sector	To generate a profit, to grow and to survive.
Voluntary sector	To provide for the benefit of the community, overcome a market failure and achieve environmental goals.

4   Identify the seven Ps of marketing.

P...

P...

P...

P...

P...

P...

P...

5   SMART targets are set by businesses so that objectives and goals can be measured. Read the following descriptions and match them to the term.

Term	Description
Specific	If the specific outcome is capable of being met.
Measurable	If the target can be achieved within a specific frame.
Achievable	When key statements are made relevant to an individual's performance.
Relevant	When appropriate targets are set by the employer.
Timebound	When the key aspects of performance must be quantified.

6   Fill in the gaps to complete the definitions. Use the list of words below.

> functions   priorities   performance   senior   roles
> delegate   executive   strategic   operations   management

There are several different .... within a business that have different ....
and various responsibilities. A .... board will consist of an executive and non-executive
director. The .... team will set the .... direction for the business, as
well as set the .... The .... leadership team will be responsible for the
operational and strategic planning, as well as the .... management of the business.
It will .... responsibility to specific teams with managers within the business and then
oversee the business ....

1 Business context part 1: sections 1.1–1.6

Short-answer exam-style practice questions

1. If a business fails, the owner is responsible for all its debts and may also lose their possessions. What key term is this describing? (1 mark)

    A A loss

    B Limited liability

    C Profit margins

    D Unlimited liability

2. Identify which of the following is an advantage of being a franchise. (1 mark)

    A The business is owned and controlled by the owner

    B The franchisor can make all the business decisions

    C The franchisor has unlimited liability

    D The risk is less as the brand is already well known

3. What does Ltd stand for? (1 mark)

    A Limited liability partnership

    B Private limited company

    C Public limited company

    D Unlimited company

4. Identify which of the following is **not** a factor that will impact a local organisation. (1 mark)

    A Time zone

    B Budget

    C Staff management

    D Internal processes

5. According to The Companies Act 2006, a 'medium' business has less than how many employees? (1 mark)

    A 10 employees

    B 200 employees

    C 250 employees

    D 50 employees

6 Which type of organisational structure is this describing: 'Managers will group employees according to their profession to enable individuals with a common expertise to work together.' (1 mark)

   A Divisional

   B Matrix

   C Flat

   D Functional

7 Identify which of the following describes a strategy for a business. (1 mark)

   A A long-term goal that has a desired overall outcome for the business

   B A detailed plan for a business with a course of action detailing the specific objectives and resources

   C Something that an organisation will want to achieve

   D A formal statement of intent

8 The Porter model has five different forces. Which of the following is **not** a force? (1 mark)

   A Bargaining power of sellers

   B Threat of substitutes

   C The threat to enter the industry

   D Competition and rivalry

9 What does CSR stand for? (1 mark)

   ....

10 Within a business, who will implement a strategic plan? (1 mark)

   ....

11 Why is the UK described as a mixed economy? (1 mark)

   ....

   ....

12 Why might it be a disadvantage for a hierarchical business to have a small span of control? (1 mark)

   ....

   ....

13 Explain the term 'egalitarian structure'. (1 mark)

   ....

   ....

1 Business context part 1: sections 1.1–1.6

14 What does MNCs stand for? (1 mark)

....

15 What is the role of Companies House? (1 mark)

....

....

16 Define the term 'vision statement'. (2 marks)

....

....

....

17 Explain the term 'networking'. (2 marks)

....

....

....

18 Name the elements included in the circular economy. (2 marks)

....

....

....

19 Unlimited liability is a feature of being a sole trader. Explain what this means. (3 marks)

....

....

....

....

20 Identify the **three** main objectives of private sector organisations. (3 marks)

....

....

....

....

> **Hint**
>
> It is important to read all of the question. Some questions will give context, followed by the question with a command word. Other questions may ask you to give some examples. Be sure to know what you are being asked before you start to answer the question.

21 Archie Carroll's corporate social responsibility (CSR) model identifies **four** different areas of responsibility. Identify each of the responsibilities. (4 marks)

> **Hint**
> This question requires you to understand a few different things. You need to know what 'corporate social responsibility' means, as well as what a model is. Underline the key elements of the question, as this will help you to write your answer. To get the marks, you have to identify the four areas of responsibility. We know there are four areas as the question tells us so. This type of question is drawing on your recall knowledge of two separate but related topics. Make sure to read all of the different parts of the question, as there may be things that help you to answer it.

....
....
....
....
....

22 A limited company is required by law to produce **two** documents. Identify these documents and describe their purpose. (4 marks)

....
....
....
....
....
....

Long-answer exam-style practice questions

1 A business has recently won a contract through a tendering process and needs to decide how to facilitate the new project. It is considering implanting a matrix structure. Evaluate the appeal of this structure to businesses who run many projects. (12 marks)

> **Plan your own answer**
> In longer exam questions, they will often provide context that includes information to set the scene and that is relevant to the question. You might be required to use specific information in this context to form part of your answer.
> ▶ Write the key themes that are identified in the question above.
> ....
> ....

1 Business context part 1: sections 1.1–1.6

- It is important that you are aware of the command word that is being used in the question so you know how to answer it. What is the command word used in this question?

  ....

- What are the features of this type of command word that you need to include in your answer?

  ....

  ....

- Now you understand the expectations of the question, write down some brief notes about the features of a matrix structure.

  ....

  ....

  ....

- Write **three** advantages of a matrix structure for the business. Make sure that you relate this to the context, which is the tendering process.

  ....

  ....

  ....

Now formulate your own answer using all the information that you have written above.

....

....

....

....

....

....

....

....

....

....

....
....
....
....
....

2 James is considering setting up his own enterprise activity using reclaimed wood collected by a friend and repurposing it into garden furniture. He has a keen interest in sustainability. James is unsure about which type of business ownership he should choose. His choices are a sole trader or beginning a partnership with a friend, who he has worked successfully with in a previous job. Analyse each form of business ownership and advise which form of business he should start.
(9 marks)

> ### Sample answer
>
> **Sole trader**
>
> James could set up as a sole trader, which means he would own and control his own business. It is easy to set up and has low set-up costs, which would be an advantage for him and his garden furniture business. James could choose his own working hours and he would be able to make all his own decisions. It will be a risk for James to start up on his own, as sole traders often fail and it is difficult for a business to grow. It can be harder to gain financial support from banks and, of course, a sole trader has unlimited liability. This means he would lose any money that he invests in the business if it were to fail. He might also lose anything else he owns depending on the amount of debt he was in from the business failing.
>
> **Partnership**
>
> James knows that he works well with his friend as they have worked together in a previous job, so they could form a partnership. A partnership is a business that is owned and controlled by two or more individuals. If James formed a partnership with his friend, they would both invest money into the business. They would also bring different skills and attributes to help create a successful partnership. The business may grow quicker with more investment. They could share their ideas, discuss any issues or important decisions together and take joint responsibility. It would be a risk to set up the partnership but this risk is shared. A partnership still has unlimited liability, which is a disadvantage. Also, a major disadvantage could be that they have disagreements in the partnership, which could result in the business ending.
>
> ### Comment
>
> Look at the answer above and consider the following questions:
>
> ▶ Does the learner work meet the command word?
>
> ....
>
> ▶ What are the strengths of this answer?
>
> ....
>
> ....

1 Business context part 1: sections 1.1–1.6

▶ What are the weaknesses of the answer?

....

....

▶ How many marks would you award the answer?

....

> **Hint**
>
> It is important to answer all aspects of the question. In the sample answer above, the learner's response is good but they have not advised which form of business James should start. If that had been included, and was appropriate, full marks could have been awarded. It is important to highlight all aspects of the question.

3 Zebra Products has been a successful high street business for many years in its local area. The business marketed itself as an ethical business by sourcing its products from a range of different locations. However, some of its products have been exposed as not being ethically sourced in a recent newspaper article. This has had a direct impact on the business. Discuss how this negative publicity could impact on Zebra Products's business. (6 marks)

....

....

....

....

....

....

....

....

> **Hint**
>
> If a question includes the name of the business in the question, it is asking you to answer the question within the context. Try to use as much information as you can from the question. However, just mentioning the name of the business in your answer will not gain you context marks as you are required to mention something specific from the question and apply it in your answer.

....

....

....

....

4 A business that was a sole trader has recently expanded to become a private limited company. It has taken on more staff and is planning to expand into new markets within the next five years. It wants to set KPIs and make its strategies more formal. Due to the expansion, the business is having to make changes to its current provision and has spent time with the new heads of department. They will be responsible for setting KPIs for the employees within their functional areas. Discuss the link between KPIs and strategies. (12 marks)

5 Discuss how a business can be monitored through the use of both internal and external audits. (9 marks)

2 Business context part 2: sections 1.7–1.11

Recall activities

1 Identify the common internal and external stakeholders in a business from the list below and fill in the diagram:

- suppliers
- employees
- managers
- creditors
- local community
- owners
- investors
- shareholders
- trade unions
- customers
- government
- board members

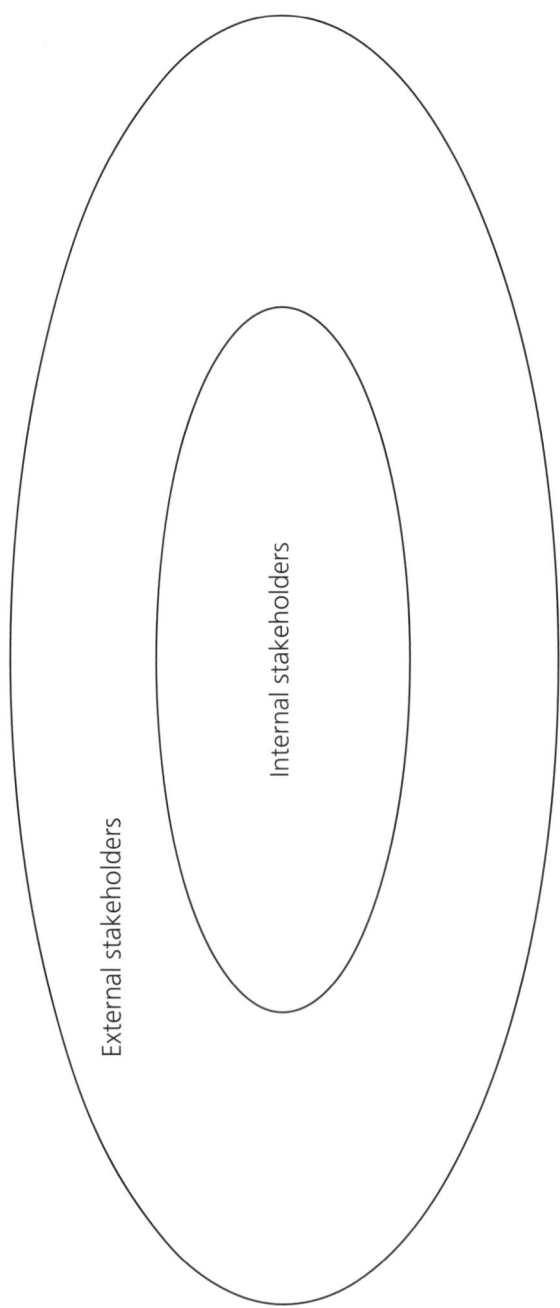

2 Business context part 2: sections 1.7–1.11

2 Complete the crossword based on different methods and channels of communication.

ACROSS

4. A method of finding out vast amounts of information using technology (8 words).

7. Teams is an example of this type of communication method (17 words).

8. Often a formal way of communicating important documents to individuals, for example, contracts (7 words).

DOWN

1. A fast, cheap and electronic method of communicating via the internet (5 words).

2. A method of speaking to a person (6 words).

3. A method of speaking face to face and directly to an individual in a quick way (9 words).

5. An internal system that provides departments with specific documents relevant to the business (8 words).

6. An informal way of communicating via mobile or a Chatbox (9 words).

3 Identify which of the following is a framework or a regulatory body.

- ▷ Information Commissioner's Office
- ▷ Health and Safety Executive
- ▷ Health and Safety at Work etc. Act 1974
- ▷ Anti-competitive regulations
- ▷ Consumer protection legislation
- ▷ Crown Prosecution Service
- ▷ General Data Protection Regulation (GDPR)
- ▷ Equality Act 2010
- ▷ Equality Advisory Support Service
- ▷ Equality and Human Rights Commission

Framework	Regulatory body

Short-answer exam-style practice questions

> **Hint**
>
> One- and two-mark questions require you to make one or two points to answer the question. They do not require much detail, will be quick to answer and will often involve you recalling knowledge rather than applying knowledge to a context.

1 Identify **one** impact on business of current and emerging digital technologies. (1 mark)

....

....

2 What does GDPR stand for? (1 mark)

....

3 Identify **one** example of an organisational value. (1 mark)

....

4 Identify **one** example of a type of governance. (1 mark)

....

2 Business context part 2: sections 1.7–1.11

5 Name **one** type of internal stakeholder. (1 mark)

....

6 Identify a method for how a business can reinforce its organisational culture and values externally. (1 mark)

....

7 Name **one** method of communication that a business will use on a regular basis. (1 mark)

....

8 Describe virtual reality. (2 marks)

....

....

9 Define 'transformation'. (2 marks)

....

....

10 Identify **one** method that a business can use to ensure that it is complying with frameworks. (1 mark)

....

11 Identify **two** examples of how a business can keep up to date with emerging technologies. (2 marks)

....

....

12 Explain the term 'mission statement'. (2 marks)

....

....

13 Describe the security considerations that an organisation should consider when it introduces a new technology to the business. (2 marks)

....

....

14 Identify what a business can do to reinforce their culture and values internally to the organisation. (2 marks)

....

....

....

Photocopying prohibited

15 Explain the term 'whistleblower'. (2 marks)

....
....
....
....

16 Identify the main differences between direct and indirect discrimination. (2 marks)

....
....
....
....

17 Explain the term 'big data'. (2 marks)

....
....
....

> **Hint**
>
> This question is only worth two marks, so you do not need to go into much detail. If you spend too much time including unnecessary detail, you may not have time to answer the other questions. Be aware of the number of marks for each question, as well the number of answer lines, as that will give you an indication of the level of detail required.

18 Explain the term 'netiquette'. (1 mark)

....
....

19 Explain the difference between formal and informal communication methods. Include examples to explain your answer. (4 marks)

....
....
....
....

2 Business context part 2: sections 1.7–1.11

20 Stakeholders are a key part of a business. Explain how communities and environmental campaigners can have an influence over the operation of a business. (4 marks)

> **Hint**
> This question has two elements to it. First, you need to identify the types of stakeholders that have been identified in the question and demonstrate your knowledge of the two different aspects (communities and environmental campaigners). Finally, you need to demonstrate how they can influence a business. There is a link between these two groups which you should be able to identify. The examiner will be looking for this in your answer.

....
....
....
....
....
....
....
....
....
....
....
....

21 Explain the term 'remote working'. (4 marks)

> **Sample answer**
> Working from home, or remote working, is a flexible working arrangement that allows an employee to work from a remote location outside of an organisation's offices, such as at home. Digital technology has made it possible to access internal systems from elsewhere and meetings can be conducted online rather than in the office. Remote working was common during the Covid-19 pandemic and continues to be a working option for many.
>
> **Comment**
> ▶ What do you think about this answer? Does the learner explain the term remote working?
>
> ....
> ....
>
> ▶ Why do you think this?
>
> ....
> ....

22 Why is it important to check and proofread correspondence before sending written communications? Explain using examples. (4 marks)

....

....

....

....

....

....

....

> **Sample answer**
>
> Any communication will give an impression of a business. If an email with incorrect information has been sent out, the person receiving the communication may gain a negative view of the business. Having a negative view may affect the confidence the person has of the business operations, which could then result in a cancellation of an order, for example. The information, tone and professionalism of the correspondence is vital for future interactions with the business.
>
> **Comment**
>
> This answer highlights the importance of accuracy when writing an email. It focuses on the negative impacts which is key. The question asks for an explanation with examples but only one example has been given. To make this answer stronger, and to gain full marks, the learner needs to include another example.

23 How does the National Cyber Security Centre help businesses? Explain your answer. (4 marks)

....

....

....

....

....

....

....

....

2 Business context part 2: sections 1.7–1.11

24 It is important to maintain professional etiquette when emailing on behalf of a business. Identify the key advice you would give to a new employee when writing a professional email. (4 marks)

....

....

....

....

....

....

....

....

25 Identify the **three** aspects of the digital process. (3 marks)

....

....

....

26 Explain how artificial intelligence (AI) could help a supermarket with customer orders. (4 marks)

....

....

....

....

....

....

27 Explain how internal and external branding can be applied to a business. (4 marks)

....

....

....

....

....

....

Management and Administration T Level Exam Practice Workbook

Long-answer exam-style practice questions

1. At a recent management meeting, the CEO of the business highlighted the importance of the company's culture and values. They want this to be demonstrated in all areas of the business and have asked teams to investigate this further. Evaluate how businesses can reinforce their culture and values to stakeholders. (12 marks)

   Plan your own answer
   - Highlight the key pieces of information in the question.
   - Write down everything you know about culture and values.

   Culture = ...

   ....

   ....

   ....

   ....

   Values = ...

   ....

   ....

   ....

   ....

   - See if you can remember the elements of the Cultural Web (1992) by Gerry Johnson and Kevan Scholes.

   (Diagram: six empty circles connected to a central circle labelled "Culture")

2 Business context part 2: sections 1.7–1.11

▶ Write a list of internal and external general stakeholders of a business.

Internal	External
....	....
....	....
....	....
....	....

▶ Now consider how your understanding of values and cultures will have an impact on some of the identified stakeholders.

....

....

....

....

▶ You will need to provide a conclusion to your answer, so come up with an evaluative statement to summarise your points.

....

....

....

Using all the information that you have completed above, compose your 12 mark answer. There are more answer lines on the next page if you need them.

....

....

....

....

....

....

....

....

....

....

....

Photocopying prohibited

....
....
....
....
....
....

2 A business wants to review the public external communication channels that it uses. They are concerned about how much time their employees are spending on social media while at work and want to introduce new protocols. Discuss what it will need to consider and provide suitable advice, using video conferencing and social media as examples. (12 marks)

> **Plan your own answer**
>
> ▶ Write an introductory paragraph to start your answer.
>
> ....
> ....
> ....
> ....
>
> ▶ Write some notes relating to advice on video conferencing.
>
> ....
> ....
> ....
> ....
> ....
> ....
>
> ▶ Write some notes relating to advice on social media.
>
> ....
> ....
> ....
> ....
> ....
> ....

2 Business context part 2: sections 1.7–1.11

▶ Now write a conclusion.

....
....
....
....

Sample answer

Read the following answer from a student. Indicators have been included to show where they have gained marks.

Technology has made it easy to communicate with people from all around the world at any time [1 Knowledge]. It means that someone in the UK can send an email to a colleague in the USA, which they can open at an appropriate time. However, this convenience can often lead people to make embarrassing mistakes that can damage their professional reputation as well as the business's. [1 Application].

Video conferencing is now an established method of meeting individuals or groups virtually [1 Knowledge]. A business should ensure that their employees are on time for meetings, are dressed appropriately, use people's names when known, use positive body language, demonstrate active listening and always thank people for their time at the end of the interaction [2 Application and Context]. These expectations could be introduced as a new policy for employees [1 Application].

Social media is another form of public external communication that could be a concern for a business. The reach of social media can be wide, powerful and quick [1 Knowledge]. It can be used for a product or service launch, a public announcement, or a networking event to involve clients and customers. It also allows businesses to use influencers to persuade potential customers to buy certain products [1 Knowledge]. Managers should produce guidance on posting on the business's social media account to ensure that no mistakes are made that could negatively impact the business. A social media post can spread far and wide very quickly and can leave a footprint that may be hard to correct or remove in the future [1 Application]. A business should also produce guidance on personal social media accounts, as a colleague could become aware of what an individual within the business does via their social media [1 Application]. They should consider carefully whether adding a manager/boss/colleague as a friend on social media is appropriate, as the employee may not want them to know about their personal life. It would also be good to produce guidance on sharing posts and checking whether the source of information is fake or not [1 Application]. A business would be advised to provide suitable guidance so that all employees are aware of the expectations when working for the business.

Comment

This student has made a good attempt at this question. The introduction is relevant to the question that has been asked. They go on to discuss video conferencing and make this relevant by giving guidance to a business about employee expectations. These are all suitable. The student then goes on to address the issues surrounding social media – both for a business and for personal accounts. Again, the advice given is suitable and demonstrates the knowledge that the student has on the topics. The weakest part of the answer is the very short conclusion at the end. Maybe they ran out of time. They would be advised to review the question again and put elements of this into their conclusion. It would have been appropriate to add some detail about how the new protocols could have been introduced.

3 Evaluate the importance of frameworks on a business. (9 marks)

> **Hint**
> Make sure that you are clear about the differences between regulatory bodies and frameworks, so you do not get confused between the two. This question focuses on frameworks, which does include legislation.

4 A technology company is introducing a new project to the team. It will need to consider which form of formal digital communication channel it is going to use to keep key internal individuals updated on the progress of the project. Evaluate different methods that could be used and recommend which one it should adopt. (12 marks)

> **Hint**
> This has a context and two different command words. Make sure you demonstrate the required skills to answer the question in full.

3 People

Recall activities

1. Match the different elements of Maslow's Hierarchy of Needs to the examples of an employer's provision for its employees.

Maslow's needs
Physiological
Security
Belongingness
Esteem
Self-actualisation

Examples of what the employer could provide
Job security.
A friendly and encouraging team so staff feel they belong.
Salary, food/drinks and sometimes accommodation.
Challenges and new opportunities for employees.
Acknowledgement of successes and opportunities to succeed.

2. Coaching and mentoring are different skills. Complete the table to demonstrate the benefits that mentoring and coaching can have on a business.

Mentoring	Coaching

3. Identify different recruitment channels and add them to the mind map.

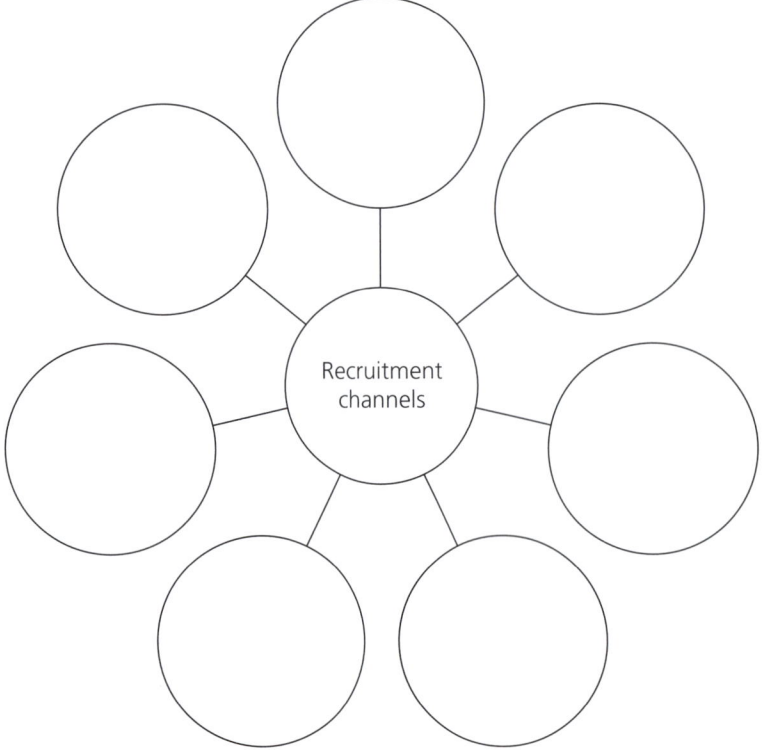

4 Match the following terms with the definitions.

Term	Definition
Value	All individuals are equal in opportunities, rights or status.
Equality	When individuals are from a range of social and ethnic backgrounds, genders, beliefs and sexual orientations.
Benefit	The advantages to a business.
Diversity	How important a particular element of a business is to the company.

5 Identify the different forms of organisational structure.

a

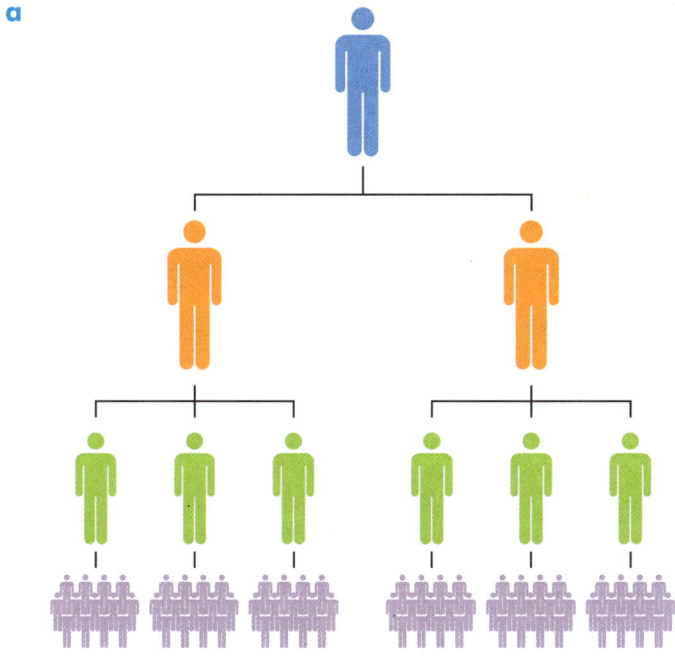

....

b

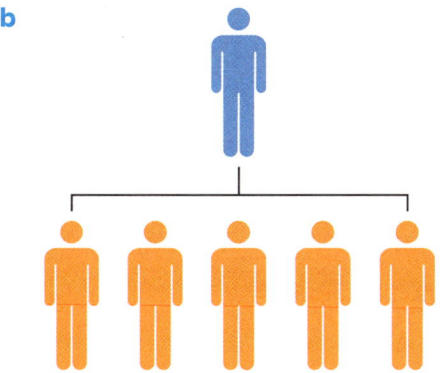

....

c

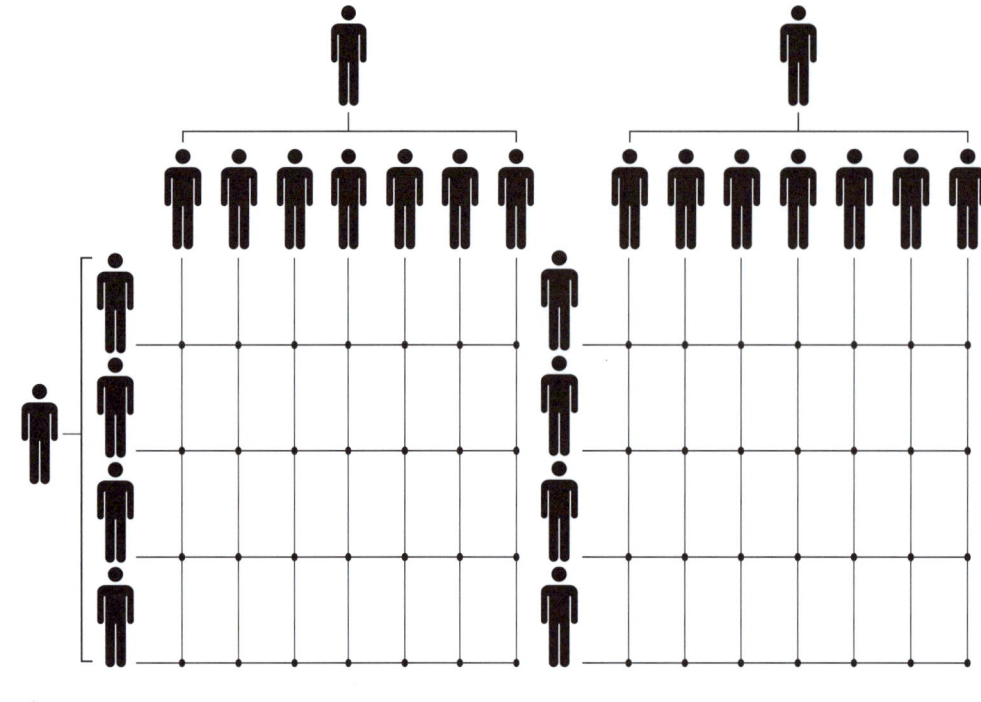

....

Short-answer exam-style practice questions

1. 'A team is not a bunch of people with job titles, but a congregation of individuals, each of whom has a role that is understood by other members.' Which model does this refer to? (1 mark)

....

2. An employee arrives at work under the influence of alcohol. What would be the business's process be for this situation? (2 marks)

....

....

....

3. Identify **one** document that is used in the recruitment process. (1 mark)

....

4. Identify **one** type of wellbeing initiative that a business could provide for its employees. (1 mark)

....

5. Explain the differences between management styles and leaderships styles. (2 marks)

....

....

3 People

6 Identify **two** different ways that a business could inform team members of the plans and progress of a new project. (2 marks)

....

....

....

7 Identify **two** different forms of employment contracts that may be offered within a business. (2 marks)

....

....

8 In a recruitment process, what can a business do to ensure that the recruitment is fair, transparent and consistent for all who apply? (2 marks)

....

....

....

....

9 Identify **two** elements of the Employment Rights Act 1996. (2 marks)

....

....

....

10 Explain how the Working Time Regulations 1998 protects employees. (2 marks)

....

....

....

....

> **Hint**
>
> It is important that you identify an exception in your answer to gain the full two marks.

11 Why would a business start disciplinary action? (2 marks)

....

....

....

12 Identify **two** methods of internal recruitment. (2 marks)

....

....

13 Explain the term 'conflict'. (2 marks)

....

....

14 State **four** of the protected characteristics of the Equality Act 2010. (4 marks)

....

....

....

....

15 Explain the participative management style. (4 marks)

....

....

....

....

....

....

....

16 Having an equal, diverse and inclusive workforce can benefit an organisation. Why would this strengthen a team? Explain your answer. (4 marks)

> **Hint**
>
> This question has three different elements to it. Firstly, you need to draw upon your knowledge of an equal, diverse and inclusive workforce. Secondly, you need to think about why having these elements will strengthen a team. Finally, you need to explain it. If you are able to combine all elements together, the examiner will be able to reward you with the marks.

> **Sample answer**
>
> Having a good mix of individuals working together means that the business can focus on the strengths and interests of each person rather than their weaknesses. This will provide a good balance and make a good team. Strengths could include: communication, problem solving, numeracy, leadership, decision making, conflict resolution and IT.
>
> **Comment**
> ▶ Has this student understood the three elements of the question as discussed in the hint above?
>
> ....

> ▶ What do you consider to be the strengths of this answer?
>
> ....
>
> ....
>
> ....
>
> ▶ What do you consider to be the weaknesses of this answer?
>
> ....
>
> ....
>
> ....

Using your comments above, write your own answer to the question.

....

....

....

....

....

....

....

....

17 Explain the onboarding process of the Employee Life Cycle. (4 marks)

....

....

....

....

....

18 Describe **two** personality groups in Belbin's team building theory. (4 marks)

> **Hint**
>
> This question focuses on the personality groups rather than the roles of Belbin's team building theory. It is important that you read the question in full as this could be seen as a trick question, which many people could answer by describing two roles rather than personality groups.

19 A business which operates internationally may have a different approach to recruitment. Identify and explain **one** approach. (4 marks)

Long-answer exam-style practice questions

1 Why is a matrix structure appealing to a business who bid for tenders to run a variety of different projects? (9 marks)

> **Plan your own answer**
>
> ▶ This question has a context. Write down below the context below.
>
> ▶ Identify the topic area of this question.
>
> ▶ You need to ensure that the examiner can see the knowledge that you have of matrix structures and that you also understand how they work. Write down the knowledge you have of matrix structures.

3 People

▶ Finally, you now need to explain why this is appealing to a business (so what happens after the project has finished?). This will be your conclusion.

....

....

....

....

Using your comments above, write your final answer to this question.

....

....

....

....

....

....

....

....

....

....

....

....

Sample answer

Look at the following answer that has been written by a student.

Matrix structures are becoming more popular due to the changes in our working patterns. Businesses will use this form if they successfully bid for a project. When the project is won, a team of specialists is brought in to complete the project, which will be headed up by the project manager. When the project is completed, the team will be broken up to fulfil other projects. Often a matrix will need support from other areas within the business, which could include finance, human resources or marketing.

How many marks would you award this response?

....

> **Comment**
>
> How the marks were awarded:
>
> Matrix structures are becoming more popular due to the changes in our working patterns [1]. Businesses will use this form if they successfully bid for a project [1]. When the project is won, a team of specialists is brought in [1] to complete the project, which will be headed up by the project manager [1]. When the project is completed, the team will be broken up [1] to fulfil other projects [1]. Often a matrix will need support from other areas within the business, which could include finance, human resources or marketing [1].
>
> Seven marks were awarded to this candidate. The learner has been able to demonstrate their knowledge of matrix structures and apply this to businesses. However, the response did lack a conclusion, which impacted on the marks that could be awarded.

2. TB Designs employs 20 employees. It has recently expanded, so team working is new to the organisation. Describe the benefits of team working to the new team at TB Designs. (12 marks)

3 JT sandwiches has expanded and opened some new stores. The business needs to devise a new induction programme for the newly-appointed managers of its stores. Devise a simple induction programme that will be held at the head office of the business. (12 marks)

4 Quality and compliance

Recall activities

1 Fill in the gaps to complete the names of these organisations.

   a I........................ O........................ for S........................

   b E................ F................ for Q............ M........................

   c B............ S................ I................

2 What does PDSA mean in terms of quality improvement?

   P..

   D..

   S..

   A..

3 Identify the regulatory body associated with the healthcare sector.

   ....

Short-answer exam-style practice questions

1 Define quality assurance. (1 mark)

2 Who are quality standards set by? (1 mark)

3 Explain why quality audits are completed. (2 marks)

4 Explain why customer satisfaction is an important aspect of quality. (2 marks)

4 Quality and compliance

5 What does TQM stand for? (2 marks)

....

6 Identify **two** advantages of improving and maintaining quality in an organisation. (2 marks)

....

....

7 Explain why a business that improves and maintains its quality standards might see a reduction in costs. (2 marks)

....

....

....

....

8 Describe the term 'accountability'. (2 marks)

....

....

....

....

9 Identify why a complaints handling process would benefit a business. (2 marks)

....

....

....

....

10 Define a trade association. (2 marks)

....

....

....

11 Describe quality improvement. (2 marks)

....

....

....

12 Define the term 'timeframe'. (1 mark)

....

....

13 Kaizen is a concept that focuses on improving things for a business. Explain how Kaizen can improve businesses. (4 marks)

> **Sample answer**
> Look at the following answer that has been written by a student.
>
> The Kaizen method focuses on the elimination of waste in a business. It seeks to improve the productivity and efficiency within the workforce. It does this by making small and effective improvements in the culture of the organisation, as well as the working practices of the business.
>
> How many marks would you award the answer? Explain why.
>
> ....
>
> ....
>
> **Comment**
> This student has clearly demonstrated their knowledge of Kaizen. They have stated the main focus of the method – eliminating waste, improving productivity and improving efficiency for the business. They also have stated how they do this and the impact the Kaizen method can have. It is a good answer and would gain the full 4 marks.

14 Explain **one** type of people-based accreditation that a business can apply for. (4 marks)

> **Plan your own answer**
> ▶ What command word is used in this question?
>
> ....
>
> ▶ The examiner wants to know your knowledge of accreditation that can be obtained by a business. Identify a people-based accreditation.
>
> ....
>
> ▶ You now need to explain Investors in People and why it is important to a business.
>
> ....
>
> ....
>
> ....
>
> ....
>
> ....

4 Quality and compliance

15 Explain the EFQM Excellence Model. (4 marks)

....
....
....
....
....
....

> **Hint**
>
> To answer this question, you need to demonstrate your knowledge of the EFQM Excellence Model. You may have to answer questions on models or theories, so it is important that you are familiar with these aspects of the specification.

16 There are three different types of quality audit. Explain **one** form of quality audit. (4 marks)

....
....
....
....

17 Describe the term 'monopoly'. (2 marks)

....
....

18 Why may process improvements occur in a business? Explain using an example. (4 marks)

....
....
....
....
....

19 Explain why it is important for a business to have a complaints handling procedure. (4 marks)

....
....
....
....
....

Long-answer exam-style practice questions

1. A catering business is about to be taken over by new owners. The new owners are aware that the business has had issues in the past and there was a period of time when it was closed by regulators. The reputation of the business has been damaged and the new owners want to build trust with its customer base. Discuss the powers that regulatory authorities have with regard to businesses. (12 marks)

> **Hint**
>
> It is important to read all of the question. Some questions will provide context, followed by the question with a command word. Other questions may ask you to give some examples. Be sure to know what you are being asked before you start to answer the question.

Sample answer

Look at the following answer that has been written by a student.

Regulators have three different ways to enforce their power over an organisation if they are not complying with the required standards for their sector. Prohibition notices can be issued if an inspector sees evidence that could present a risk to others. A prohibition notice will mean that the current activities will be stopped immediately and will not be allowed to continue until the risk has been removed. This will require the business to change its working practices within a specified period of time set by the inspector and it will then be reinspected before the business can resume. Another action that a regulatory authority could impose is closure. This is completed in serious situations and will require a business to close with immediate effect for often 48 hours so that the issues can be fixed. Again, the business will have to be reinspected at a later date with the business remaining closed until then. In extreme cases, the regulator will apply to the Magistrates' court for a longer closure period. This could result in a permanent closure in extreme circumstances. The final power that a regulator can have over a business is suspension. When a business is suspended, it cannot operate during the suspension time period. During this time, the regulators will investigate the issues that have led to this suspension and determine if they were deliberate, accidental or just through carelessness. After the investigations have taken place, the business will be informed of the changes that need to be made to reopen or will be issued with a permanent closure notice.

How many marks would you award this response?

....

Comment

This answer received full marks, as it answered the question very well, with the learner demonstrating good knowledge and application.

How the marks were awarded:

Regulators have three different ways to enforce their power over an organisation if they are not complying with the required standards for their sector. Prohibition notices can be issued if an inspector sees evidence that could present a risk to others [1]. A prohibition notice will mean that the current activities will be stopped immediately [1] and will not be allowed to continue until the risk has been removed [1]. This will require the business to change its working practices within a specified period of time set by the inspector [1], which then will be reinspected before the business can resume [1]. Another action that a regulatory authority could impose is closure [1]. This is completed in serious situations and will require a business to close with immediate effect for often 48 hours so that the issues can be fixed [1].

4 Quality and compliance

> Again, these will have to be reinspected at a later date with the business remaining closed until then. In extreme cases, the regulator will apply to the Magistrates' court for a longer closure period [1]. This could result in a permanent closure in extreme circumstances [1]. The final power that a regulator can have over a business is suspension. When a business is suspended, it cannot operate during the suspension time period [1]. During this time, the regulators will investigate the issues that have led to this suspension and determine if they were deliberate, accidental or just through carelessness [1]. After the investigations have taken place, the business will be informed of the changes that need to be made to re-open or will be issued with a permanent closure notice [1].

2 An organisation is considering applying for a quality accreditation. Evaluate how this organisation could benefit from obtaining a quality accreditation. (12 marks)

Plan your own answer

▶ What command word is used in this question?

....

▶ With this type of command word, what do you need to ensure you include?

....
....
....

▶ Define a quality accreditation.

....
....
....

▶ Can you think of an example of a quality accreditation that you could include in your answer?

....
....

▶ Write some advantages for a business in obtaining a quality accreditation. You should aim to write at least three advantages (benefits). This is because if one is not relevant, you still have two others that are hopefully suitable. You need to justify these.

....
....
....
....
....
....

▶ It is important within an evaluate answer that you come to a reasoned decision to conclude your answer. For this answer, you want to persuade the organisation to now work towards gaining a quality accreditation. Write a conclusion below.

....
....
....
....
....
....
....

Using all the information above, formulate your whole answer to the question.

....
....
....
....
....
....
....
....
....
....
....
....
....
....
....
....
....

3 Assess the implications on a business for non-compliance with regulatory authorities. (12 marks)

4 Discuss how implementing a quality standard can improve a business. (12 marks)

> **Hint**
>
> Any question related to improvements or impacts will need you to discuss these within your answer. It is important that you relate this to the business or the context that has been provided. The impacts must be business related, for example, why having a quality standard is positive for a business and how it will make it better.

5 Finance

Recall activities

1 Match the financial terms to the descriptions.

Term	Description
Sales turnover	The level of output at which total costs equal total revenue. This is the point at which a business makes no profit or no loss.
Accounting period	The total amount of money received for all goods and/or services that a business has sold in a given time period, for example, a year.
Break-even point	Tax that is set by the government on the net profit of a limited company.
Corporation tax	Details the revenue (money) that comes into a business from the sales of products or services, as well as expenses that the business has used.
Retained profit	The time period (annual, quarterly or monthly) covered by a report or set of accounts produced by a business.
Income statement	This is a financial statement that details the organisation's financial position, including what the organisation owns and what it owes other organisations and individuals.
Balance sheet	Tax that a government puts on its working population based on the salary/wages that employees earn.
Income tax	An amount of the net profit that a business has left to keep in its accounts after all other costs and payments have been paid.

2 Fill in the gaps using the words below.

| suppliers | track | financial | countries | reporting | investors |
| comply | opportunity | leaders | penalties | imprisonment | judge |

……………………… reporting is important to the business. This is because its customers, ……………………… and the government need to know the financial elements of the business. A business will need to ………………………, analyse and report on its financial activities. It also needs to ……………………… with the law in the UK and other ……………………… regarding the requirement of financial reporting. If it does not obey, a business may face financial ……………………… and, in extreme cases, ……………………… for non-compliance with the law. Accurate financial reports will be looked at by ………………………, employees or customers of the business so that they are aware of the performance of the business. By ……………………… the health of the business, this helps to create a comparison with other market ………………………, giving a snapshot of its metrics. This means that the business can measure itself by tracking its progress to ……………………… its performance against the metrics. Businesses often will use reporting as an ……………………… to drive the business forward.

3 Complete the following crossword using the clues provided.

Across

2. Debts that a business may have incurred while trading (11 words).

5. An amount of money that a business may charge to customers or owe to other businesses (5 words).

6. The business owner's reward for investing in the business organisation (6 words).

9. The amount of money that is within a business's financial account (7 words).

Down

1. Items that an organisation owns that have a value (6 words).

3. When the finance officer reviews the accounts and, if required, adjusts them (10 words).

4. When the total costs that the business has to pay are more than the revenue the business earns from selling its products and services (4 words).

7. The money that a business makes from selling its products and services (7 words).

8. Value added tax (3 words).

4 What is the calculation for gross profit?

....

5 What does the net profit demonstrate?

....

Short-answer exam-style practice questions

1 Define a fixed cost. (1 mark)

2 How do you calculate break-even? (2 marks)

3 Identify **two** internal sources of finance. (2 marks)

4 Identify **two** forms of general utilities. (2 marks)

5 Identify **one** form of capital purchase that an organisation may purchase for its business. (1 mark)

6 Explain the term 'variable cost'. (2 marks)

7 Identify **two** forms of external sources of finance. (2 marks)

8 Explain the term 'variance'. (2 marks)

9 National Insurance is a payment that most people pay. Identify what this payment funds. (2 marks)

10 Explain **two** advantages of hire purchase. (2 marks)

11 What method of communication does crowdfunding rely upon? (1 mark)

12 Explain the term 'depreciation'. (1 mark)

13 Identify **two** forms of tax that small businesses and the self-employed workforce have to pay. (2 marks)

14 Explain what an overdraft is. (2 marks)

15 An annual report is an example of how management can report the performance of a business. Identify the different areas that have to be included in this document. (4 marks)

16 Why is it important that financial audits are completed on a regular basis? Explain your answer. (4 marks)

> **Hint**
> To gain full marks, it is important that you identify what an audit is and the different forms of audits (internal and external).

5 Finance

17 Explain break-even and how this information can benefit a business. (4 marks)

....
....
....
....
....
....

> **Sample answer**
> Look at the following answer that has been written by a student.
>
> Break-even is the level of output at which total costs equal total revenue. At this point, a business makes no profit and no loss. A business needs this information because it needs to understand how many products or services it has to sell at a given price to break-even. Break-even also helps with decisions the business needs to make, which could include the unit sales price, sales targets, pricing strategies and sales forecasts.
>
> How many marks would you award this response?
>
> ....
>
> **Comment**
> This is a good answer to the question. The student demonstrates their understanding of break-even and goes on to explain how break-even can help a business in terms of decision-making, as well as understanding the selling targets they have to meet. It would be awarded the full marks of 4 marks.

18 Produce an income statement for a Drinks Carts company using the following figures. (4 marks)

Sales	£156,400	Cost of sales	£80200
Rent	£20,000	Advertising	£7000
Equipment	£150	Uniforms	£100
General expenses	£7000	Computers	£300

Income Statement for Drinks Cart

£   £

> **Hint**
> With any question that involves numbers, make sure that you use all of the numbers in the correct order. Tick each number off so you know what you have used so you do not miss anything. It is important to know what you need to add and subtract.

19 Explain why spend authorisations are important in business. (4 marks)

....

....

....

....

....

....

20 Identify **four** areas of financial reporting. (4 marks)

....

....

....

....

....

....

21 Explain how reputational risk can impact a business. (4 marks)

....

....

....

....

....

....

22 Cash flow statements are split into three different activities. Describe **two** of the activities. (4 marks)

....

....

....

....

....

....

5 Finance

23 Explain why there are disadvantages to a business using the owner's capital to fund a new project. (4 marks)

....

....

....

....

....

....

....

24 Identify **four** areas that will be included in a financial summary report. (4 marks)

....

....

....

....

....

....

....

25 Identify **two** internal and **two** external risks that can impact on the financial stability of a business. (4 marks)

....

....

....

....

....

....

....

....

Long-answer exam-style practice questions

1. A successful Midlands-based business is looking to open more outlets in other areas of the UK. It will need to raise finance in order to expand its operations. It is considering a bank loan or angel investors. Advise the business on the different ways of financing its expansion. (12 marks)

   Plan your own answer

   ▶ This is a context-based question. Identify the key elements from the question.

   ▶ What command word has been used in the question?

   ▶ Considering the command word, what will your answer need to demonstrate?

   ▶ Write down all the information that you know about bank loans.

   ▶ Write down all the information that you know about angel investors.

   ▶ Now you have written lots of information about a bank loan and angel investors, which would you recommend? Why is this?

5 Finance

Using all the information that you have completed above, answer the question in full.

2 Discuss why a business should monitor its revenue against its expenditure on a regular basis. (12 marks)

> **Sample answer**
> Look at the following answer that has been written by a student.
>
> The reason that a business should monitor its revenue against expenditure is to discover any risks that could mean the expenditure may exceed the revenue. This means that the business will be spending more than it can afford. Completing regular financial risk assessments will mean if financial changes occur, such as an increase in interest rates, the business can ensure that it can afford to operate. By tracking revenue and expenditure, the business will know its financial health. Other risks could include reputational risk. This is when a business's operation is damaged, which could result in losing customers and a loss of stakeholder and shareholder confidence. If customers lose confidence in the business, they will go elsewhere, which will directly affect sales and profits. Financial difficulties can result in the business owing more money than it is bringing in as revenue, which will impact on its business operations. The consequences of not monitoring a business's revenue against its expenditure can impact very quickly on a business, so it is important that the financial management of the business is good so it can continue to operate in the future.
>
> How many marks would you award this response?
>
> ....
>
> **Comment**
> How the marks were awarded:
>
> The reason that a business should monitor its revenue against expenditure is to discover any risks [1] that could mean the expenditure may exceed the revenue [1]. This means that the business will be spending more than it can afford [1]. Completing regular financial risk assessments will mean if financial changes occur, such as an increase in interest rates, the business can ensure that it can afford to operate [1]. By tracking revenue and expenditure, the business will know its financial health [1]. Other risks could include reputational risk [1]. This is when a business's operation is damaged, which could result in losing customers and a loss of stakeholder and shareholder confidence [1]. If customers lose confidence in the business, they will go elsewhere, which will directly affect sales and profits [1]. Financial difficulties can result in the business owing more money [1] than it is bringing in as revenue, which will impact on its business operations [1]. The consequences of not monitoring a business's revenue against its expenditure can impact very quickly on a business [1], so it is important that the financial management of the business is good so it can continue to operate in the future.
>
> This is a good attempt at the question. The student has outlined the consequences of not monitoring a business's revenue against its expenditure. It was awarded 11 out of 12 marks, as the conclusion does not really add much to the answer.

5 Finance

3 Balance is a small business that specialises in fitness. It has been operating for two years, during which time the business has grown to offer a full range of different exercise and fitness classes for all ages. It wants to add a gym with up-to-date equipment to attract more customers. In order to fund this, it will need finance. Evaluate two different finance options and recommend the one that will be best for the business. (12 marks)

> **Hint**
>
> Recommending or making a decision will often be part of a question. In order to gain the marks, you must justify the decision, which means presenting an argument of why the decision or recommendation is appropriate for the business. Try to use the context if one is provided and use detail from the context to back up your decision/recommendation.

4 Ollie owns a fruit and vegetable market stall. He has built up a large and loyal customer base, which has increased each year by 10 per cent. During the pandemic, he noticed that some regular customers were not buying from the stall and decided he would supply and deliver any leftover stock to the local customers who could not purchase from him. He is thinking about expanding to a fruit and veg delivery business. He needs to work out the break-even point to help with his decision-making. Using the figures below, work out the break-even point and advise Ollie if it is a viable option. (9 marks)

Fixed costs: £4,000 per year

Variable costs: £5.00 per box

Selling price per box: £15.00 per box

> **Hint**
>
> Always check your calculations carefully as it is very easy to make mistakes when you are in the exam and under time pressure. It can help if you estimate an answer first, as that way you can tell if, for example, you have added too many zeros or put the decimal point in the wrong place.

6 Policies and procedures

Recall activities

1. Match the following policies and procedures terms to the descriptions.

Term	Description
RAG rating	Formal guidance that explains why tasks have to be completed in a certain way.
Metrics	A set of rules that employees are expected to follow while at work.
Code of conducts	Traffic light system that demonstrates a level of concern for a business.
RIDDOR	Quantitative information that a business can use to measure the progress against its overall objectives.
Policy	Reporting of Injuries, Diseases and Dangerous Occurrences Regulations.

2. The Health and Safety at Work etc. Act 1974 has a number of requirements for a business to ensure that everyone is safe. Whose responsibility is it within the business to ensure this is followed?

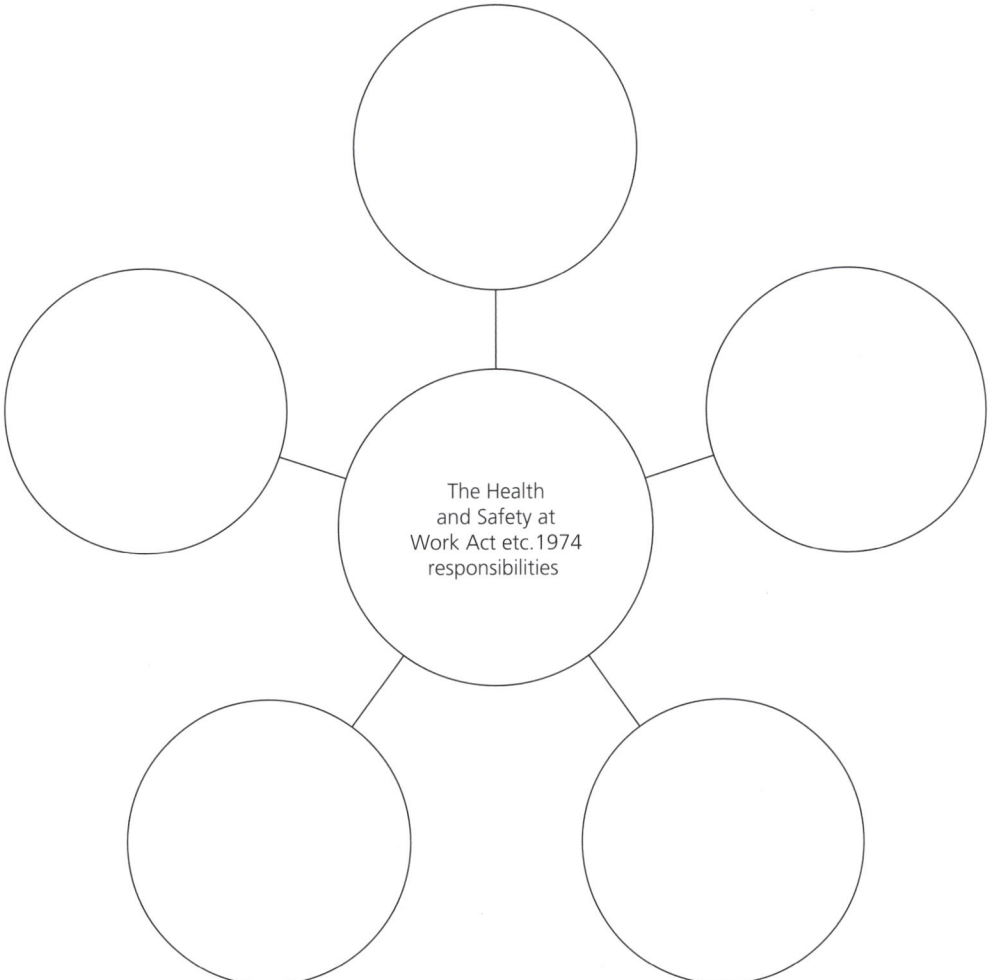

3 There are nine protected characteristics under the Equality Act 2010. Fill in the missing ones.

Age
Disability
Gender reassignment
Race
Sexual orientation

Short-answer exam-style practice questions

1 Identify **three** different types of policies that would be found within an organisation. (3 marks)

....

....

....

2 Explain the difference between mandatory and non-mandatory policies and procedures. (2 marks)

....

....

....

....

3 Explain why businesses use KPIs. (2 marks)

....

....

....

4 Explain what a RAG rating is for. (3 marks)

....

....

....

....

6 Policies and procedures

5 Identify the main difference between a process and a procedure. (2 marks)

....

....

6 Within a large organisation, who will create the sickness policy? (1 mark)

....

7 Identify **one** policy and procedure that is required by law. (1 mark)

....

8 Explain why version control is important when developing a policy or procedure. (2 marks)

....

....

9 Describe the term 'metrics'. (2 marks)

....

....

10 Identify **one** form of metrics that a business can use to measure success. (1 mark)

....

11 Describe how the impacts of a procedure will be assessed. (4 marks)

> **Sample answer**
>
> A business will want to assess the impacts of a procedure in order to evaluate its effectiveness. KPIs will enable the business to look at various metrics, such as customer satisfaction and the growth of the business. These can be tracked on a regular basis and improvements made when required. Another assessment tool that could be used is data analysis in the form of sales, as this can determine if a new procedure based on selling products is working. Using these assessments will enable a business to help make decisions as the business moves forward.
>
> **Comment**
>
> ▶ Has the student addressed the command word? Explain your answer.
>
> ....
>
> ....
>
> ....
>
> ▶ How many impacts have they identified and what are they?
>
> ....
>
> ....
>
> ....

> ▶ Do you think that theses impacts are appropriate for the question?
>
> ....
>
> ....
>
> ▶ How many marks would you award this answer out of four?
>
> ....

12 Describe the purpose of both policies and procedures within a business. (4 marks)

....

....

....

....

....

....

....

> **Hint**
>
> It is important to know the difference between a policy and a procedure in order to answer this question fully. If your answer demonstrates that you are unclear, you may not receive full marks for your answer.

13 Explain the main differences between a flexible and inflexible policy. (4 marks)

> **Hint**
>
> An explain question wants you to give a reason, so it is important that you include this as part of your answer.

....

....

....

....

....

14 Identify **two** characteristics of a procedure. (2 marks)

....

....

....

6 Policies and procedures

15 How can policies and procedures support consistent workflows? (4 marks)

16 Explain the potential positive impact of a new policy on the staff within a business. (2 marks)

17 Explain the main differences between a strategic and a financial KPI. (4 marks)

18 Explain how businesses use KPIs to monitor performance. (4 marks)

Long-answer exam-style practice questions

1 Describe how a policy is developed. (9 marks)

> **Sample answer**
> Look at the following answer that has been written by a student.
>
> A business will need to determine if there is a need for a policy in the first place. It may be required because of a change in the law or particular regulations related to the sector that the business operates in. Once this is established, the business will need to justify its reasons so budget can be allocated for the time and money that it will take to complete the policy process. The role of leader will need to be allocated, with this person having overall accountability for the policy. They will have to have the right skill set to be able to fulfil the role and also to be able to liaise with stakeholders regarding the policy when it is being researched and developed. Once the policy has been written it will need to be approved by management before it is implemented into the organisation.
>
> How many marks would you award this response?
>
> ....
>
> **Comment**
> How the marks would be awarded:
>
> A business will need to determine if there is a need for a policy in the first place [1]. It may be required because of a change in the law or particular regulations [1] related to the sector that the business operates in. Once this is established, the business will need to justify its reasons [1] so budget can be allocated for the time and money that it will take to complete the policy process [1]. The role of leader will need to be allocated [1] with this person having overall accountability [1] for the policy. They will have to have the right skill set to be able to fulfil the role [1] and also to be able to liaise with stakeholders [1] regarding the policy when it is being researched and developed [1]. Once the policy has been written it will need to be approved by management [1] before it is implemented into the organisation.
>
> This is a good example of how a question should be answered. The answer describes various aspects of a policy, with the student demonstrating their good knowledge of the topic area. It would be awarded the full 9 marks.

2 Examine how organisations use performance monitoring processes to measure achievements. (9 marks)

> **Plan your own answer**
> ▶ Which command word has been used in this question?
>
> ....
>
> ▶ What are the **two** key elements that the questions focuses on?
>
> ....
>
> ....

6 Policies and procedures

▶ Write down the key points of the first element that you have identified.

....
....
....
....
....

▶ Write down the key points of the second element that you have identified within the question.

....
....
....
....
....

▶ Now you have identified the two key areas with various points, formulate these into sentences to form part of your answer.

....
....
....
....
....
....
....
....

▶ Now try to conclude your answer to the question.

....
....
....
....
....

Management and Administration T Level Exam Practice Workbook

3   A large business has recently merged with another organisation. There have been several organisational changes, which include alterations to some policies and procedures. Evaluate the impact of policies and procedures on staff and organisations. (12 marks)

> **Hint**
>
> In any evaluation question, it is important that you provide a justification, which is an argument to demonstrate that the correct decision has been made.

4 Key Performance Indicators give businesses focus and direction. Discuss how KPIs could be cascaded to staff. (12 marks)

7 Project and change management

Recall activities

1 A PESTLE analysis stands for:

P..

E..

S..

T..

L..

E..

2 Match the project and change management terms to the descriptions.

Term	Description
PRINCE2 project management methodology	The process is known as the 8 Step Model of Change.
ADKAR model	This theory looks at the science behind persuading individuals to make the right decision without them realising.
Kübler-Ross theory	This model Illustrated the three processes of change using the concept of changing the shape of a block of ice.
McKinsey 7S model	This model explores seven different phases of improving performance or managing change within a business by dividing the elements into two different categories (hard and soft elements).
Nudge theory	Awareness, desire, knowledge, ability and reinforcement are all elements of the five stages of change.
Lewin's Change Management Model	Denial, anger, bargaining, depression and acceptance are all the emotions that individuals go through when change is considered and during the introduction phase, the implementation and finally the new normal.
Six Sigma	This is a common business methodology that aims to improve the different processes a business uses, reduce waste and errors, and increase customer satisfaction throughout the business. It is predominately based on data and statistical analysis.
Kotter change management theory	This involves projects in controlled environments. The main principles of the methodology focus on the management of resources and risks within a business by dividing projects into different stages with clearly defined roles and responsibilities for the individuals involved.
SCRUM	Focuses on the project lifecycle by breaking down large projects into smaller chunks, meaning that teams can produce work faster to optimise their workflow and focus on continuous improvements to reduce errors.
Agile project management	It encourages individuals to think in a particular way in order to get work completed. The thinking concerns continuously improving and adjusting to the fluctuations in various factors.

7 Project and change management

3 Fill in the gaps using the words below.

> competitive   forward   efficiency   improve   operations
> improvements   service   technological   customer   innovative

Businesses do not stay still. It is important for them to keep moving .... A business will do this so that it can remain .... and continue to improve, which could involve being .... Continuous improvements mean that a business looks at its current provision and seeks to .... what it is doing in terms of products/services and processes. This is important so that a business does not get left behind or become irrelevant and therefore have to close due to lack of sales and profits. As well as making continuous ...., a business will want to look at how innovation could improve aspects of the business. Innovation could be a product, a ...., a strategy or a business model that is useful to the business and is often unique to the area of business it operates in. Innovation could involve a new .... aspect that enhances the business's operations. Innovation enables a business to adapt its ...., encourages growth and if the innovation is unique, it could mean that it makes its business stand out from other competitors. Innovation can help a business to improve .... and productivity, increase profit, potentially gain new customers, increase .... retention and improve the quality of products and services.

4 Complete the diagram based on the different stages of the project lifecycle.

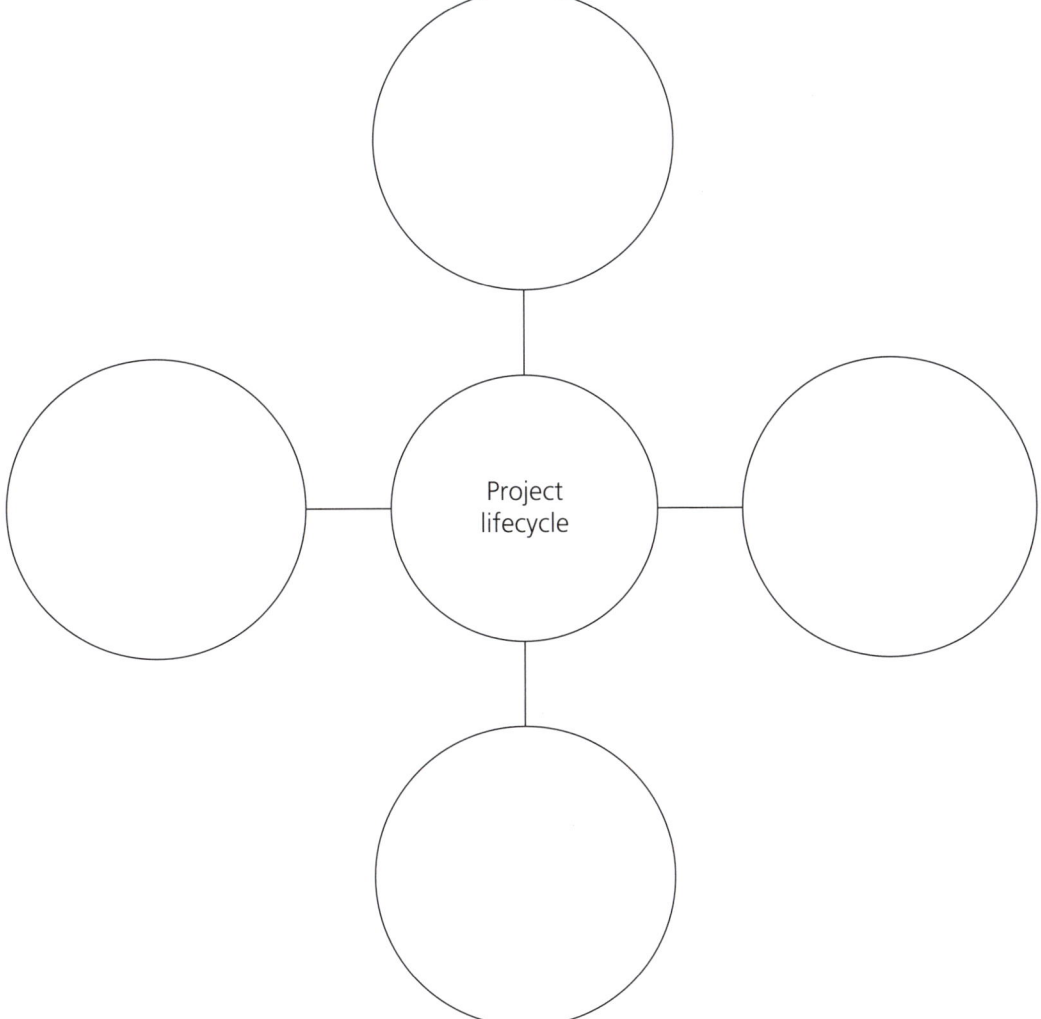

Short-answer exam-style practice questions

1 Define project management. (2 marks)

2 What does PERT stand for? (1 mark)

3 Explain why a project initiation document is important for a business. (1 mark)

4 Identify **two** questions that could provide context for a project. (2 marks)

5 Identify the **three** elements of research. (1 mark)

6 Explain the meaning of continuous improvements for business. (2 marks)

7 Why is it important to embrace change in business? (2 marks)

7 Project and change management

8 Explain the difference between qualitative and quantitative data. (2 marks)

....
....
....
....

9 Define the term 'project postmortem'. (2 marks)

....
....

10 Explain the phrase 'dynamic environment'. (2 marks)

....
....

11 Explain the main difference between a model compared to a theory. (2 marks)

....
....

12 Explain why there might be resistance to change within a business. (2 marks)

....
....
....
....

13 Identify **two** of the stages of project management. (2 marks)

....
....

14 Explain the term 'resource management'. (2 marks)

....
....
....
....

15 Identify **two** areas of resource management. (2 marks)

....
....

16 Explain the phrase 'web analytics'. (2 marks)

....

....

17 Explain why a business would complete a field trial. (2 marks)

....

....

18 Explain the term 'conclusion'. (2 marks)

....

....

19 A SWOT analysis can be used to develop a strategy for a business. Explain the different elements of a SWOT analysis. (4 marks)

....

....

....

....

....

....

....

Sample answer

Strengths: These are the internal elements of the business that it completes well.

Weaknesses: These are the internal elements that the business does not do well and which can affect its performance.

Opportunities: These are the external elements of the business that the business could benefit from implementing in the future.

Threats: These are the external elements that the business does not have control over but can affect how it operates.

Comment

This learner has been able to identify the four different elements of a SWOT analysis. They have also been able to identify the internal and external elements of the SWOT analysis that are related to the business. This is important as internal elements can be controlled compared to external elements. An example of an extra element would be changes in government policies; if any new legislation is implemented, this will need to be introduced by businesses. The learner then goes on to explain each element of the SWOT analysis successfully. It is in the required detail as the maximum number of marks the learner can gain for this question is 4.

7 Project and change management

20 Explain a project management tool. (4 marks)

....
....
....
....
....
....
....

21 Describe the plan-on-a-page concept. (2 marks)

> **Hint**
>
> For a describe question, you have to give an account of a topic that includes the relevant characteristics, qualities or events of the subject. It is best to give two or three points in your answer depending on the number of marks that are available for the question.

....
....
....
....
....
....

22 Explain the difference between a conclusion and a project postmortem. (4 marks)

....
....
....
....
....
....
....
....

> **Sample answer**
>
> A conclusion is a summary of the key points that have been discovered as a result of completing the specific research or project evaluation. It enables a business to give final thoughts on the most important aspects. This will aid decision-making about what is to happen next. A project postmortem evaluates whether a project was successful or not in meeting the business's goals. A project postmortem can be a meeting or report.
>
> **Comment**
>
> The answer provided by this student would be awarded full marks. This is because they have clearly identified the main differences between a conclusion and a project postmortem and have then gone on to explain these, relating it to the context of a project.

23 Explain the difference between a project management tool and a project management approach. (4 marks)

....

....

....

....

....

....

....

24 A business is considering diversifying its business operations into a new market. Explain how a PESTLE analysis can help the business when considering change. (4 marks)

> **Hint**
>
> Make sure you revise a range of different models, theories and principles so that you know them in sufficient depth and understand the differences between them.

....

....

....

....

....

....

....

7 Project and change management

25 Explain the advantages of the Pareto principle. (4 marks)

....

....

....

....

....

....

....

....

26 Explain why evaluation is a key part of projects. (4 marks)

....

....

....

....

....

....

....

27 Explain **one** advantage of having a dashboard as a form of project management. (2 marks)

....

....

....

....

28 Explain the detail provided by flow charts. (4 marks)

....

....

....

....

....

....

....

Management and Administration T Level Exam Practice Workbook

Long-answer exam-style practice questions

1. Discuss how innovation can improve a business. (9 marks)

> **Sample answer**
> Look at the following answer that has been written by a student.
>
> Innovation enables a business to set new goals, which means that it can continue to operate and hopefully be relevant for many years to come. Being relevant means that the business's products and services are needed and wanted within the market. Innovation could involve a new technological aspect that enhances the business's operations, or an upgrade to a different system that makes things quicker for the business, which could revolutionise an aspect of the industry. Innovation can help a business to adapt its operations by encouraging growth and, if the innovation is unique, it could mean that it makes the business stand out from competitors. Innovation can enable a business to improve efficiency and productivity, increase profit, potentially gain new customers, increase customer retention and improve the quality of its products and services.
>
> How many marks would you award this response?
>
> ....
>
> **Comment**
> How the marks would be awarded:
>
> Innovation enables a business to set new goals [1], which means that it can continue to operate and hopefully be relevant for many years to come [1]. Being relevant means that the business's products and services are needed and wanted within the market [1]. Innovation could involve a new technological aspect that enhances the business's operations [1], or an upgrade to a different system that makes things quicker for the business, which could revolutionise an aspect of the industry [1]. Innovation can help a business to adapt its operations [1] by encouraging growth [1], and if the innovation is unique, it could mean that it makes the business stand out from competitors [1]. Innovation can enable a business to improve efficiency and productivity, increase profit, potentially gain new customers, increase customer retention and improve the quality of its products and services [1].
>
> This is a good example of a response to this question. It would be awarded 9 marks. The learner has clearly understood the term innovation and been able to explain well how innovation can be good for a business by using different examples. They have a good conclusion.

2. A company wants to evaluate its current portfolio of products and services that it produces. Evaluate a range of different methods that it could use. (9 marks)

> **Plan your own answer**
> ▶ Identify the key points from this question.
>
> ....
>
> ▶ Identify some different methods that the business could use.
>
> ....
>
> ....

7 Project and change management

▶ Select two methods that you feel confident in explaining and write a few sentences on each below.

....
....
....
....
....
....

▶ Now conclude your answer.

....
....
....
....

Now formulate your own answer using all the information that you have written above.

....
....
....
....
....
....
....
....
....
....
....
....
....
....

3 A business is considering changing its staff catering area. It needs to use a visual project management tool and have selected critical flow analysis. Evaluate this tool. (12 marks)

7 Project and change management

4 A business that has predominantly had a workforce working from home has realised that it needs staff to now work in its offices. It knows that there will be resistance to this change as staff are happy working in this way. The managing director has heard that the ADKAR model focuses on employees, which she feels would be a good model to adopt. She needs to know more information about it. Discuss the ADKAR model and if it would be relevant for this scenario.
(12 marks)

8 Business behaviours

Recall activities

1. Decide which of the following is a verbal or non-verbal form of communication.

   ▷ posture
   ▷ tone
   ▷ gestures
   ▷ eye contact
   ▷ voice projection
   ▷ clarity of voice
   ▷ facial expressions

Verbal	Non-verbal

2. Fill in the gaps using the words below.

   | individual | engaged | listening | active | neutral | work | positive |

   .... listening is a form of communication when an individual is .... in a conversation with another individual in a .... way. It involves .... to another person, paraphrasing or reflecting back what they say, making sure that you remain .... with your responses so that the .... will continue to share their thoughts. Active listening works well within social, home and .... situations.

3 Complete the mind map on different forms of advertising that a business could use to promote its products and services.

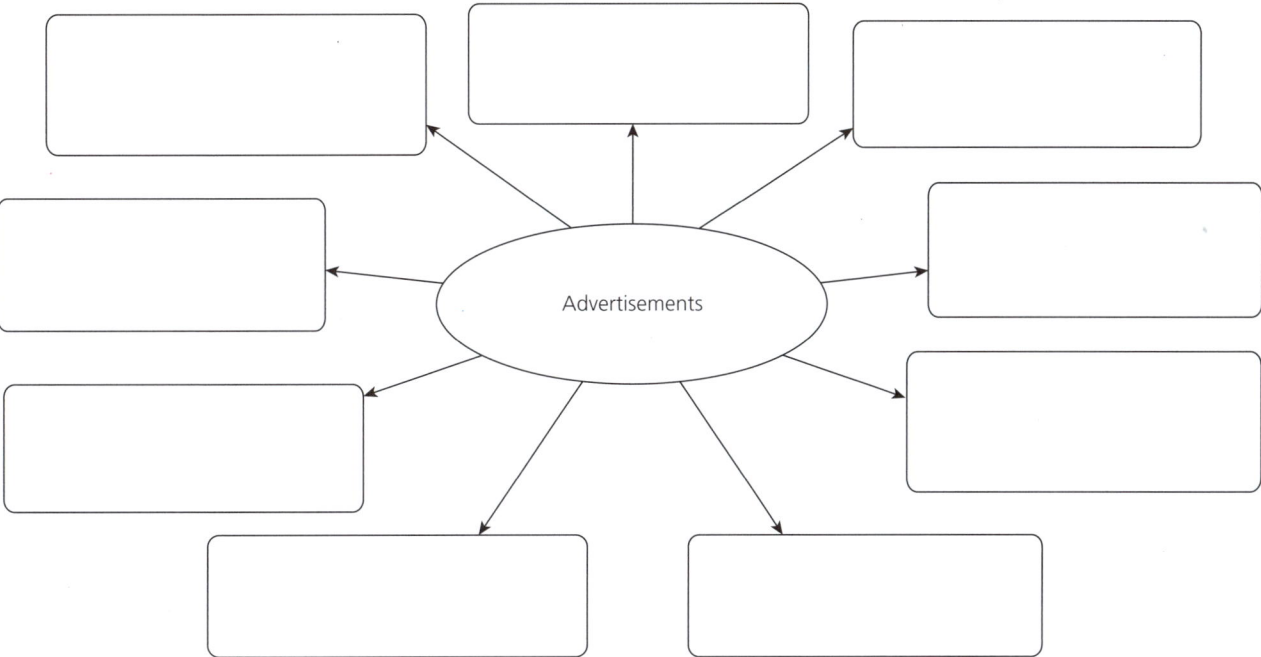

4 Match the written forms of communication to the correct definitions.

Term	Description
Form	This enables businesses to attach a range of different documents that the receiver will then be able to access when it is convenient for them. It enables stakeholders to communicate with each other worldwide without having to consider time differences.
Report	This form of communication gives businesses the opportunity to sell their products or services to customers. Some forms of communication are purely for the users to gain information about a particular topic that they are interested in.
Memo	The user of this communication can share videos, photos and view things that interest them. Businesses can promote themselves using this communication method by sharing and linking posts to their business.
Website	Businesses may require employees to complete a document that is written or online, requiring the user to provide information which could be personal.
Email	Within a business organisation, specific areas will need to provide a progress update on different tasks. This could be in the form of project updates, functional area updates, employee performance reports, financial documents, etc.
Social media	This form of communication is a short document that is prepared and sent to internal employees of an organisation.

5 Complete the following crossword based on marketing communication.

Across

2. A large poster on the side of a building that can be seen by passers-by (10 words).

4. A way of advertising a business's products or services throughout the world online (8 words).

5. Businesses promote their products through a mobile phone provider (7 words).

6. Promoting a brand towards a potential customer in a very obvious way (13 words).

7. Informing a customer about a product so they are motivated to buy it (13 words).

8. These are digital platforms where information can be accessed by the user at their own convenience (8 words).

Down

1. Handed out to people in the street to advertise products and services (6 words).

3. Businesses pay to promote products or services in different forms which include TV, cinema, newspapers and magazines (14 words).

6 Integrity is described as how a business conducts itself to demonstrate its honesty and high moral principles. Trust is how individuals are able to believe in the reliability of a business and its operations. Read the following words and decide if they are examples of integrity or trust.

▷ honesty
▷ being reliable
▷ showing commitment
▷ openness
▷ strong moral principles
▷ dependable
▷ honest communication

Integrity	Trust

Short-answer exam-style practice questions

1 What type of communication is an infographic? (1 mark)

....

2 How many pillars of resilience are there? (1 mark)

....

3 What does CPD stand for? (1 mark)

....

4 Explain the difference between adaptability and flexibility. (2 marks)

....

....

....

....

5 Identify and explain **one** method of prioritisation that is used within businesses. (2 marks)

....

....

....

6 List the **three** elements of a feedback sandwich. (3 marks)

....

....

....

7 Explain the term 'business policy' and how it is linked to a business procedure. (4 marks)

....

....

....

....

8 Identify **three** different ways of demonstrating integrity in the workplace. (3 marks)

....

....

....

9 Define the term 'rapport'. (1 mark)

....

....

10 As a manager, part of the role is to be accountable. Outline what the term means and explain the positive elements of being accountable. (4 marks)

> **Plan your own answer**
>
> ▶ This question has two different parts to it. It also has two elements to the question. Identify the two separate parts.
>
> Part 1:
>
> ....
>
> Part 2:
>
> ....
>
> ▶ What are the two different elements to the question?
>
> First element of the question:
>
> ....
>
> Second element of the question:
>
> ....

8 Business behaviours

▶ Now that you know what you are being asked, outline what accountable means. You need to make two points.

....
....
....

▶ Now explain the positive elements of being accountable, making sure that you relate this to being a manager.

....
....
....
....

Now formulate your own answer using all the information that you have written above.

....
....
....
....
....

Compare your answer to the sample answer below.

Sample answer

Accountability means that an individual or individuals will take responsibility for the work that they have completed. If there are positive or negative outcomes to the work, they will be liable for the outcomes and then will need to act upon them. When managing a team, the manager will be accountable for the overall goals that the team are set. Being accountable can improve relationships, job satisfaction and empowerment, and can also lead to promotions.

11 Recognition and reward can help to promote behaviour change. Describe how this could be used in a large retail store. (4 marks)

....
....
....
....

Hint

This is another 4-mark question so use a similar approach to the one you have just completed to answer this question.

12 Identify **four** forms of communication that a business may use. (4 marks)

....

....

....

....

13 Identify **two** non-verbal methods of communication. (2 marks)

....

....

....

14 Identify the alternative name of digital billboards. (1 mark)

....

15 Explain the term 'interactive content'. (2 marks)

....

....

....

16 Identify the **three** As of active listening. (3 marks)

....

Long-answer exam-style practice questions

1 Managers within an organisation have become concerned about how teams are working. Having worked from home for a number of years, the employees are now returning to the office on a regular basis. It is clear that the teams are not acting with integrity and have not built trust with each other due to working from home. This is clearly demonstrated in the way that they work. The business needs to change this. Evaluate the importance of integrity and building trust for the benefit of the business and working with colleagues. (12 marks)

8 Business behaviours

Plan your own answer

▶ Read the question and highlight the key areas of the text above to help you focus on what you are being asked.

▶ Identify the command word that has been used in the question.

....

▶ Firstly, you need to demonstrate your knowledge of integrity and building trust. Complete the mind maps to identify the key elements of integrity and building trust.

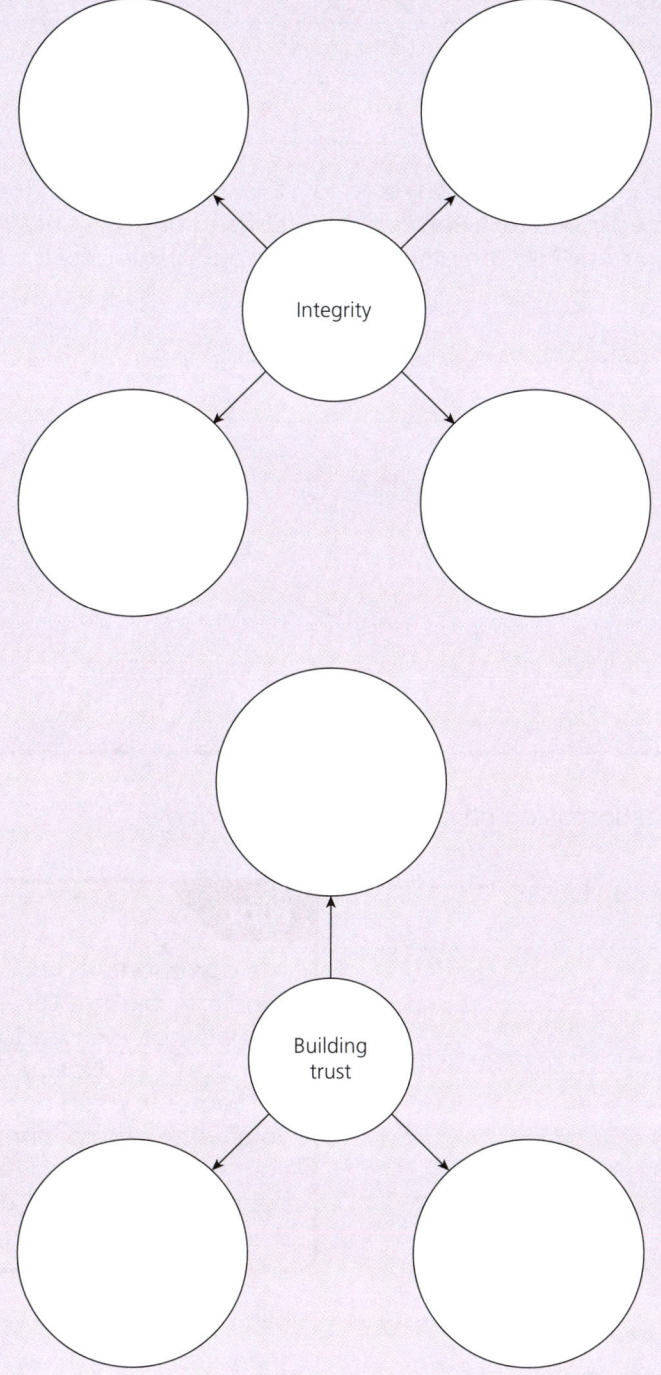

▶ Using the notes from your mind maps, put the key points into sentences to demonstrate your knowledge of the two areas covered in the question.

....
....
....
....
....
....
....

▶ Now that you have demonstrated your knowledge, you need to make this relevant to the context using the key words highlighted in the text. Remember it focused on individuals working from home and then coming back into the office, and their lack of integrity and trust within the team.

....
....
....
....
....
....
....
....

Write your full answer to the 12-mark question using all of the information above.

....
....
....
....
....
....
....
....

> **Hint**
>
> The command word used is 'evaluate'. This means that you need to make a qualitative judgement based on your written factors from your knowledge and the context. You need to reach a specific conclusion.

Compare your answer to the sample answer below.

> **Sample answer**
>
> Integrity and trust are important qualities that should be demonstrated within the workplace [1] on a daily basis, as individuals can then show that they are responsible, reliable and honest people who can complete their job role as an individual within a team [1]. Having trust with colleagues means that through good and honest communication, if an issue does arise, an individual can be open about their feeling towards a task [1] that they may be finding difficult. This could then be resolved as a team [1]. If a workplace does not have this support, then this could be an issue for the business [1]. Integrity helps improve engagement from all [1], which could result in more sales [1], decisions could be made more easily [1], closer links could be made within the team and the overall business reputation could also be improved [1]. Therefore, it is vital that the business ensures that all employees understand the importance of integrity and building trust [1]. The business will also need to recognise the impact of working from home for extended time scales and the reintroduction of office working [1]. They could implement compulsory CPD activities to help with this aspect, which then could be implemented and reviewed at different points [1]. Hopefully these various positive steps will help the business to have a workforce that has more integrity and that has built trust with each other to benefit all.
>
> **Comment**
>
> This learner was awarded 12 marks, as the answer demonstrates that they have a good knowledge of integrity and building trust. They have also been able refer to the context and build this into their answer by stating the positive elements of engagement. They have ended their answer with some ways that the business could make the situation better for all.

2 A business wants to formalise the CPD process that its employees complete within the business. Many employees have attended internal and external training events, and gained qualifications related to their work, but often managers are not aware of the new skills and qualifications within their team. Evaluate the importance of tracking the development of each employee for an organisation. (12 marks)

8 Business behaviours

3 A small local business has decided that it wants to reach a wider customer base and so it wants to sell its products online. It has no online presence. Advise and inform the business of the key elements that could help it when designing its website. (12 marks)

4 A 24-hour gym will have to close in the near future for a deep clean. It will be shut for 24 hours to allow this process to take place and this needs to be communicated to clients. Discuss the most suitable methods of communication to ensure that clients are aware of the situation. (9 marks)

Page left intentionally blank

T-LEVELS
THE NEXT LEVEL QUALIFICATION

MANAGEMENT AND ADMINISTRATION: CORE
EXAM PRACTICE WORKBOOK

Develop the vital skills you need to achieve your best in the T Level exams with this accessible and engaging Exam Practice Workbook.

➡ Review and consolidate your knowledge with varied recall activities for every topic including crosswords, quizzes and more

➡ Reinforce your understanding and boost your exam confidence with both short- and long-answer exam-style practice questions to help you break down the question

➡ Improve your exam technique with guidance on how to plan and review your responses, plus exam hints and sample student answers

Also available:

9781398372559 Management and Administration T Level: Core
9781398379268 My Revision Notes: Management and Administration T Level

'T-LEVELS' is a registered trade mark of the Department for Education.

'T Level' is a registered trade mark of the Institute for Apprenticeships and Technical Education.

The T Level Technical Qualification is a qualification approved and managed by the Institute for Apprenticeships and Technical Education.

HODDER Education
+44 (0)1235 827827
education@hachette.co.uk
www.hoddereducation.com

ISBN 978-1-0360-0703-4